Children's Authors

Margaret Wise Brown

Jill C. Wheeler
ABDO Publishing Company

visit us at
www.abdopublishing.com

Published by ABDO Publishing Company, 4940 Viking Drive, Edina, Minnesota 55435.
Copyright © 2007 by Abdo Consulting Group, Inc. International copyrights reserved in all
countries. No part of this book may be reproduced in any form without written permission from
the publisher. The Checkerboard Library™ is a trademark and logo of ABDO Publishing
Company.

Printed in the United States.

Cover Photo: Westerly Public Library
Interior Photos: Brooklyn Museum, Gift of Wallace Putnam from the Estate of Consuelo Kanaga
    p. 21; Corbis pp. 11, 15, 17; Getty Images p. 23; University Archives, Robertson Library,
    Hollins University pp. 12, 13; Westerly Public Library pp. 5, 7, 9, 19

Series Coordinator: Megan Murphy
Editors: Heidi M. Dahmes, Megan Murphy
Art Direction: Neil Klinepier

Library of Congress Cataloging-in-Publication Data

Wheeler, Jill C., 1964-
    Margaret Wise Brown / Jill C. Wheeler.
       p. cm. -- (Children's authors)
    Includes index.
    ISBN-10 1-59679-762-2
    ISBN-13 978-1-59679-762-8
    1. Brown, Margaret Wise, 1910-1952--Juvenile literature. 2. Authors, American--20th
century--Biography--Juvenile literature. I. Title. II. Series.

PS3503.R82184Z96 2006
813'.52--dc22
                                                                                2005018461

Contents

A Happy Accident

The year 1997 marked a special time for one of the most popular children's books in history. It was the 50th anniversary of *Goodnight Moon*. Since its first printing in 1947, *Goodnight Moon* has sold more than 7 million copies. As many as four generations of children have enjoyed this simple, classic story.

Goodnight Moon is a picture book about getting ready for bed. The words in early children's picture books were not thought to be very important. But *Goodnight Moon* is special. It reads like a poem.

Margaret Wise Brown wrote *Goodnight Moon*. She wrote more than 100 books during her brief career, including *The Runaway Bunny* and *The Important Book*. Brown never set out to write books for children. She called it a happy accident. Yet, she pioneered many changes in the world of children's literature.

Brown was among the first people to write about the everyday world of childhood. Her success came from her ability to bring the child within her to life. She helped create a whole new way of looking at books for young readers.

Margaret Wise Brown

Margaret in the Middle

Margaret Wise Brown was born on May 23, 1910, in Brooklyn, New York. She was the middle child of Robert Brown and Maude Johnson Brown. Baby Margaret joined her two-year-old brother, Benjamin Gratz Jr. Another daughter, Roberta, was born about two years later.

Robert and Maude had moved to New York from Missouri. Robert took a job with a company that made ropes, cords, and bags. He traveled often. Sometimes, his job took him to faraway places for a year at a time. He later became vice president and **treasurer** of the company.

Maude had hoped to be an actress one day. Instead, she ended up staying home with the children. That was very common in those days. Most women did not attend college either. Yet Maude had earned a college degree. She later insisted her daughters go to college, too.

Margaret was five years old when her family left Brooklyn. They moved to a big, new house in nearby Long Island, New York. Long Island had many beaches, woods, and wildflowers. All of the Brown children enjoyed playing outdoors. Margaret enjoyed it most of all.

Margaret at age five

A Made-up World

Margaret had a wild imagination. She and Roberta often made up plays and acted them out for their friends. Their collie, Bruce, was frequently included in their games and stories. So was their cat, Ole King Cole.

The Brown children had many other pets, too. Sometimes they had as many as 20 rabbits in cages in their backyard! Rabbits were among Margaret's favorite animals. Later, they became favorite characters in her books, too.

Growing up, Margaret and Roberta shared a bedroom. The two often talked and played games after their parents put them to bed. Sometimes, Margaret read to Roberta. Years later, Roberta realized Margaret had not been reading the actual stories. Instead, Margaret had made up her own details while staring intently at the pages.

Due to their father's job, Margaret and Roberta changed schools many times. They had attended four different schools by Margaret's seventh year of study. Those changes made it

hard to make friends. Luckily, the sisters had each other.
However, Margaret later talked about spending much of her
childhood alone. She said she often played in the "countries
of the worlds" she made up.

*Margaret (right) and Roberta (left) often included pets,
such as rabbits and Bruce the collie, in their games.*

Studying in Switzerland

Margaret was 13 years old when her father had to take another long business trip. He was assigned to go all the way to India. Robert and Maude decided to take the girls part of the way. Margaret's brother was attending a boarding school in New York. So, he did not go with them.

In 1923, the family took a ship to Europe. They visited the Netherlands and France. Then, Margaret and Roberta went to a boarding school in Switzerland. Robert and Maude boarded another ship for India.

Margaret and Roberta spent two years at the Swiss school. Classes were taught in French. The two girls were **fluent** in French when they returned to New York in 1925.

The next year, the Brown family moved to Great Neck, New York. Once again, Margaret and Roberta changed schools. They entered the Dana Hall girls' school in the same class. Margaret liked Dana Hall. The school urged all the girls to think for themselves.

In 1928, Margaret and Roberta graduated from Dana Hall. Roberta went on to study at Vassar College in Poughkeepsie, New York. Margaret chose the same college her mother had attended. It was Hollins College near Roanoke, Virginia.

Margaret and Roberta attended boarding school in Lausanne, Switzerland.

Hollins College

Hollins College had fewer than 300 female students. Margaret soon knew almost all of them. She was known by the nickname Tim, which she had received at Dana Hall. The girls thought Margaret's blond hair was the color of **timothy** hay.

School friends remembered Margaret as a one-of-a-kind person. She liked to throw silly parties. She preferred long walks outside to time in the classroom. Sometimes, she threw off her shoes and waded in the nearby creek.

Margaret enjoyed her time at Hollins College. Yet she did not always work very hard at her studies. She failed chemistry class even though she needed it to graduate. She considered dropping out of Hollins before her senior year.

In the 1920s, Hollins was a women's college. Today, the school is known as Hollins University. It now allows male students into its advanced degree programs.

Fortunately, school officials offered Margaret a chance to improve her grades. So, she tried harder during her last year and studied more than before.

That same year, Margaret wrote an essay that was published in the campus **literary** magazine. One of her teachers believed that Margaret might be a writer one day. She encouraged her to write more. This meant a lot to Margaret. She continued to stay in contact with this teacher throughout her life. Margaret even sent her a copy of her first children's book years later.

While not an excellent student, Margaret excelled at sports. At Hollins College, she was a member of the varsity field hockey team. She also participated in campus horse shows.

An Experiment in Education

Margaret graduated from Hollins College in 1932 and moved back in with her parents. She had no idea what she wanted to do. Many of her friends were getting married. But, Margaret had yet to meet someone she wanted to marry.

Margaret spent the next few years living at home. But soon, she had a plan. A friend of hers was involved with Bank Street in New York City. This was an experimental school for teachers. Margaret applied for a place in the student-teacher program there. She decided to see if teaching was something she wanted to do.

The program began in 1935. Margaret was a teacher's assistant at one of Bank Street's New York-area schools. She divided her time between studying and teaching. Margaret marveled at the imaginations of her students. She also learned a lot about the way children think, feel, and learn.

The Bank Street program was a turning point for Margaret. The school itself was unusual. It had a nursery school for very young children. Plus it had cooperating day schools for older children. The people who ran Bank Street wanted to learn as much as they could about children.

Some of the people at Bank Street were working on changing children's books, too. They explored subjects that appealed to a child's senses. They also experimented with **rhymes**, rhythms, and **repetition**. Margaret soon added children's books to the many things she was writing at the time.

Most schools wanted to turn children into little adults. But Bank Street schools were different. Teachers were urged to try to understand what childhood was like so they could help children learn better.

Better Books for Children

Brown published her first children's book, *When the Wind Blew*, in 1937. That same year, she was named editor for a new children's publishing house. Brown had completed her Bank Street studies and was excited to take on this new responsibility.

Bank Street classrooms had shown Brown that children hunger for stories about the world they live in. So as editor, she began finding authors and illustrators that would feed this desire. Plus, she wrote some stories herself.

Brown often tested the **manuscripts** and illustrations on the children at the Bank Street schools. She paid attention to their responses. She noted what word patterns and sounds they liked. It all helped her make the manuscripts better.

Brown also noticed that young children don't always treat books carefully. So, she began creating books in new **formats**. In 1938, she published a book called *Bumble Bugs*

Opposite page: *Brown wrote The Noisy Book *after watching children read. She noticed that they loved to imitate and repeat noises. The Noisy Book *lets them make noise while they read or listen to the story.

and Elephants. It was printed on sturdy, cardboard pages. Toddlers could bite it and tug on it without ruining the cover or pages.

One of Brown's most popular books was published in 1939. *The Noisy Book* is about a dog named Muffin with bandages on his eyes. The dog learns what is around him from noises the children make while reading the book.

Saying Goodnight

Brown wrote or cowrote nearly 50 books in the 1940s alone. She sold books to several different publishers. She also bought a house on an island off the coast of Maine. She called it the Only House. Brown had her own name for almost everything.

She also rented a small house in New York City. She named it Cobble Court. It was there in 1945 that Brown wrote *Goodnight Moon*. She wrote the book all in one morning.

Goodnight Moon is about a young rabbit preparing to go to sleep. The rabbit looks at all the things around him. Brown had done a similar thing before she joined Bank Street. She would wake up and look slowly at everything in the room. It helped her feel less sad when she didn't know what to do with her life.

Goodnight Moon blended Brown's poetic talents with a child's world. It became her best-known book. But, it was not popular right away. *Goodnight Moon* sold just 6,000 copies in fall 1947. Some people thought it was too **sentimental**. In fact, the New York Public Library did not own a copy until 1973!

Sometimes Brown wrote under different names. She used pen names, including Timothy Hay, Juniper Sage, and Golden MacDonald. Brown did not think an author's name mattered. It was the story that was important.

Final Chapter

Brown added to her string of children's books in the early 1950s. She also experimented with other types of children's entertainment, such as songs and musical recordings. She told friends she hoped to write for grown-ups eventually, too.

In 1952, Brown met a young man named James Rockefeller. After a few months, the two decided to get married. Brown planned to vacation in France and then join Rockefeller in Panama, where they would marry.

Brown sailed for France in September 1952. Her book *Mister Dog* had just been published in French. She brought copies to give to local children while she visited. Then on October 30, Brown suddenly fell ill. She went to a hospital in Nice, France, due to pain in her **abdomen**. The doctors operated to make the pain go away.

After the surgery, everything seemed fine. Brown was recovering well and was nearly ready to leave the hospital. Then she died suddenly. Doctors later learned that Brown had died when a blood clot in her leg moved to her brain.

Margaret Wise Brown's successful career was cut short by her unexpected death. But, her work continues to delight children. And in recent years, young readers have discovered new titles. A number of Brown's books have been published since her death, including *The Fierce Yellow Pumpkin*.

Brown loved dogs, especially Kerry blue terriers. One of her dogs was named Crispin's Crispian. He was the inspiration for the book **Mister Dog: The Dog Who Belonged to Himself.**

Glossary

abdomen - the part of the body located between the chest and the legs.

fluent - able to speak clearly and easily in a particular language.

format - the shape, size, design, or layout of printed material.

literary - of or relating to books or literature.

manuscript - a book or article written by hand or typed before being published.

repetition - the act of repeating or being repeated.

rhyme - a group of words with similar sounds.

sentimental - showing feeling or emotion.

timothy - a type of European grass that is often grown for use as hay. It is a golden color.

treasurer - a person who handles the money for a business, organization, or government.

Web Sites

To learn more about Margaret Wise Brown, visit ABDO Publishing Company on the World Wide Web at **www.abdopublishing.com**. Web sites about Brown are featured on our Book Links page. These links are routinely monitored and updated to provide the most current information available.

One of Brown's favorite pastimes was beagling. Beagling is the sport of hunting rabbits on foot with a pack of hounds. Here, Brown (right) is pictured with some of her beagling buddies.

Index